Name of this wrecker 2021 Ella

Favourite perfume 2021 Arianna Grande
2023 = eau de perfum

Shoe size 6 - 2021, 2023 = 6

Favourite song Boom clap - 2021
2023 - sex sound

Favourite singer the weeknd

Hair colour 2021 Blonde   2023 blonde

Eye colour Green

Best friend 2021 Mia   2023 Ellie

Boy/friend 2021 Frankie
2023 Harry

PAGE 1

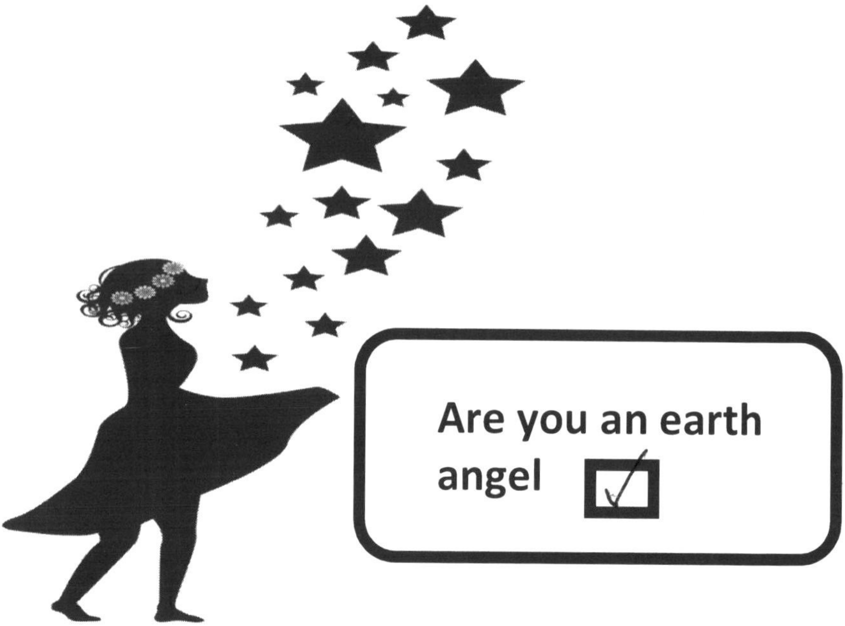
Are you an earth angel

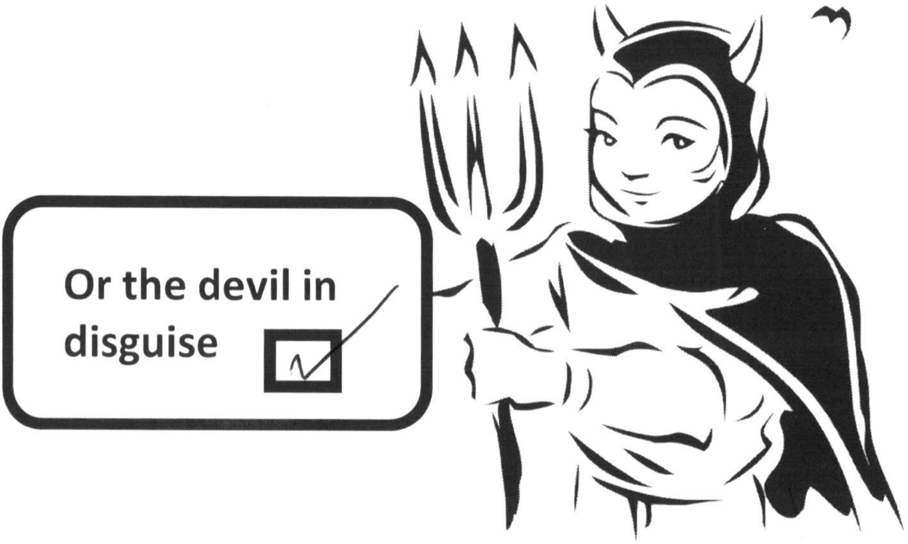
Or the devil in disguise

ITEMS NEEDED FOR TASKS

☥ toothpaste ☥   ☥ cream ☥

☥ nail varnish ☥   ☥ eye-liner ☥

☥ juicy orange ☥   ☥ lip stick ☥

☥ paint ☥   ☥ jam ☥

☥ pencil ☥   chocolate spread

☥ tomato ketchup ☥

☥ custard ☥

☥ mayo ☥

☥ you ☥

☥ your foot ☥

start from any page

get crazy

be creative

be wreckless

be funny

get dirty

forget clean! get messy

Be kind (well only if you want to)

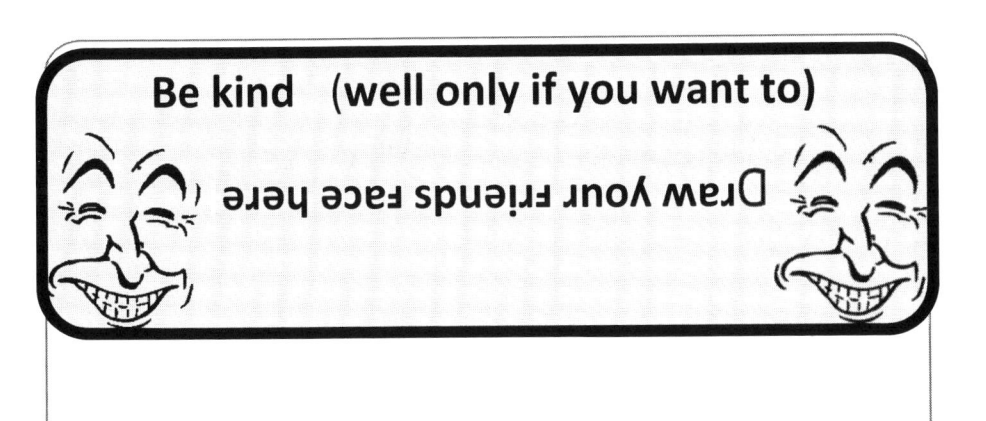

Draw your friends face here

Date: 28/10/2021

Quote Of The Day

"Be positive, their are better days in their way.

Today I am truly grateful for...

My friends and family.

Here's what would make today great...

If I had Mc'Donalds.

I am...

happy and grateful.

Some amazing things that happened today...

Nothing.

Some amazing things that happened today...

Nothing

What could I have done to make today even better?

nothing

(つ ◕‿◕)つ ♥ Naughty wrecking ideas for today 😊

> Write a wish below
> Then wreck it
> With **toothpaste**

I wish I could fly and turn invisible.

> Write your worst Friends name
> Now wreck it
> With **jam**

Charlie -

(つ ◕‿◕)つ ♥ Did you wreck it silly? 😊

(っ◕‿◕)っ ♥ Naughty wrecking ideas for today 😊

> Write your favourite colour
> Now wreck it with
> With mayo!

Baby blue

> Write your favourite Number
> Now wreck it with
> Lip balm

28

(っ◕‿◕)っ ♥ Did you wreck it silly? 😊

```
HUMAN
MALFUNCTION
WRECK THIS PAGE
I REPEAT
WRECK THIS PAGE
HUMAN AS
GONE CRAZY
```

Wreck those hearts anyway you want

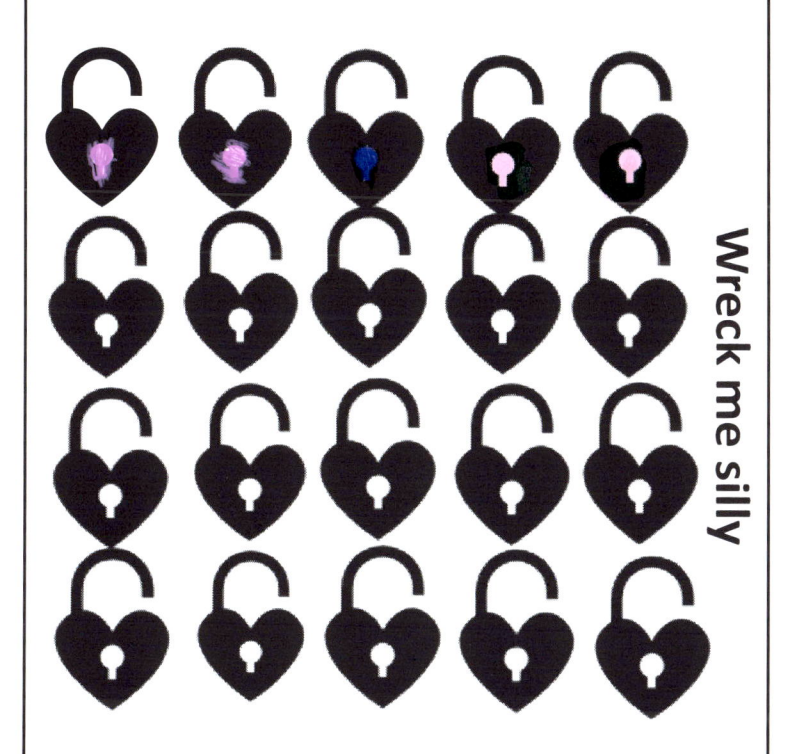

Wreck me silly

Date:

Quote Of The Day

Today I am truly grateful for...

Here's what would make today great...

I am...

Some amazing things that happened today...

Some amazing things that happened today...

What could I have done to make today even better?

Date: 4/12/2021

Quote Of The Day

"Believe in yourself"

Today I am truly grateful for...

My friends

Here's what would make today great...

I am...

Some amazing things that happened today...

Some amazing things that happened today...

What could I have done to make today even better?

BIRTHDAY REMINDER

JANUARY
- Nanny Bird
- Lance

FEBRUARY
- Rick
- Grampy

MARCH
- Skye
- Olivia
- Zach
- Nanny Julie

APRIL
- Billy
- Mia

MAY
- Phil

JUNE
- Pupper
- Maddison
- Emmy

JULY
- Mum
- Louie
- Sarah
- Cian
- Brooke

AUGUST
- Lily and Lexy
- Dad
- Leighton
- Kelly

SEPTEMBER
- Chloe
- Barrie
- Isla
- Alfie
- Evie

OCTOBER
- Me
- Anita
- Dan
- Lee
- Kerry
- Steve

NOVEMBER
- Andy
- Tash
- Anyia
- Millie

DECEMBER
- Nanny Jean

Jan- Nanny Bird's Bday.
March- Skye, Zach and Olivia's Bday.
April-

Jan- Nan - 30th   Lance - 19th

Feb- Rick - 24th   Grampy - 17th

March- Skye - 24th   Olivia - 13th   Zach - 24th
Nan - 14th

April- Billy - 12th   Mia - 24th

May- Phil - 12th

June- Papper - 2nd   Maddison - 26th
Emmy - 5th

July- Mum - 3rd   Louie - 23rd   Sarah - 15th
Cian - 16th   Brooke - 7th

August- Lily - 6th   Lexy - 6th   Leighton - 4th
Kelly - 31st   Dad - 22nd

Sept- Chloe - 24th   Isla - 10th   Alfie - 10th
Evie - 29th   Barries - 17th

Jan- Nanny Bird and Lance's Bday.

Feb- Rick and Grampy's Bday

March- Skye, Olivia, Zach and Nanny Julie's Bday.

April- Billy and Mia's Bday.

May- Grandad Phil's Bday.

June- Dapper, Maddison and Emmy's Bday.

July- Mum, Louie, Sarah, Cian and Brooke's Bday.

August- Lily, Lexy, Dad, Leighton and Kel.y's Bday.

September Chloe, Isla, Alfie, Evie and Barrie's Bday.

Oct - Me - 28th Dan - 11th Lee - 20th
      anita - 22nd kerry - 15th steve - 8th

Nov - andy - 13th tash - 10th anyia - 5th
      millie - 30th

Dec - Nan - 1st

Oct - Me, Dan, lee, kerry, Anita and Grandad Steve's Bday.

Nov - Andy, Tash, Aniya and Millie's Bday.

Dec - Nanny Jean's Bday.

Time table: week 1

	1	2	3	4	5
1 Mon	Maths G07	English F13	Photo SA	Tscience G14	Tscience G14
1 Tue	PE SH	Hsc S04	Math F03	R.S. G01	Photography SA
1 Wed	PE SH	Tscience G14	English F12	English F13	Tscience G14
1 Thur	Hsc S04	Photo SA	English F13	Math G07	Tscience F20
1 Friday	Tscience F20	Math G07	PE SH	English F13	R.S. G01

Time table week 2

	1	2	3	4	5
2 Mon	R.S G01	Tscience F20	Tscience G14	Tscience G14	Maths G07
2 Tue	Maths G07	English F13	Tscience F20	Tscience F20	R.S G01
2 Wed	English F13	Hsc S02	PE SH	Tscience G14	Maths G07
2 Thur	Photo SA	Photography SA	English F13	Tscience G14	Maths G07
2 Fri	English F13	Tscience G14	Maths G07	Hsc S02	Hsc S02

→ Triple science — Mrs Dawson, Mr Jeeva, Miss Woodward
→ Photography — Mrs McDowell, Ms Lang
→ English — Miss Luff
→ Maths — Mr Hardy
→ P.E — Miss Mahony
→ Health and social care — Miss Bulbeck
→ Religous studies — Mr Cessford

Mood Tracker

	J	F	M	A	M	J	J	A	S	O	N	D
1												
2												
3												
4												
5												
6												
7												
8												
9												
10												
11												
12												
13												
14												
15												
16												
17												
18												
19												
20												
21												
22												
23												
24												
25												
26												
27												
28												
29												
30												
31												

- → Jolly
- → cheerful
- → excited
- → awake
- → tierd
- → Happy
- → angry
- → sleepy
- → unhappy
- → Hurt
- → Depressed
- → dissapointed
- → IDK?
- → sad

Assign color and mood to a specific square and color the squares according to your mood

So pretty.
It's a shame to wreck it!

Wreck the spiders web
With tip-ex

What ya thinking

Hmm I'm thinking what is better than Mc'Donalds.
#Nothing?!

DATE 28/10/2021　　　**ROUND**

PLAYER - Ella
SCORE -

PLAYER - Billy
SCORE - 1

**Answer the questions
To wreck a balloon
Pop with a pencil?**

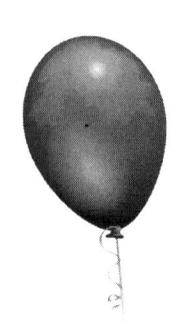

Write hello in French

...Bonjour......

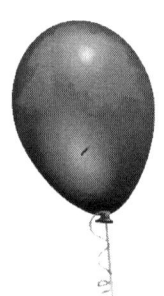

Write hello in Spanish

...Hola...........

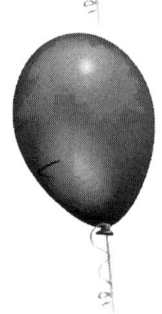

Write hello in Italian

...Ciao..........

Write hello in Russian

...ПрNBET......

Any big plans for this year?

going to lanzorote!!!
26th July
- WAS AMAZING

Colour me

Don't wreck me

Colour me silly

Make me pretty

Yes. I know it's silly but..........

Fill the shapes with the word wait for it.....
FART

Write your secrets,
cleanse your soul,
dilute your anger,
dissolve those secrets
with the help of a felt tip pen!

I don't have any secrects!

Stir the panda out
While eating a fishfinger
Sarnie!
↓Drip tomato sauce↓

Confession box

Most treasured thing in your life?
.... Family ....

Most favourite food?
.... Chips ....

Someone you love?
.... My family/friends.

What makes you happy?
.... Food ....

Favourite flavour crisps?
.... Salt and vinigar ....

Dogs or cats?
.... Dogs ....

Best childhood memory

When I ~~used~~ went a wee on Dan.
When I used to beat tia with pillows.

Worst childhood memory?

I fell of a tree on holiday.
Billy bite a whole in my back
My dad kicked me down the stairs.
I fell off a chair in Primary.

Best holiday?

Ibiza

lanzarote

Tick the boxes That apply

I am kind ☑   I am energetic ☑

I am religious ☐

I am lazy ☑

I am confident ☐

I am happy ☑   I get hurt easily ☐

I dropped a fart in public ☑

I am in love ☐   I am well behaved ☐

I love animals ☐

I love chocolate ☑

I love music ☑

1. Why do ducks have feathers?

2. What does an house wear?

3. What shorts do clouds wear?

4. Why should you never trust stairs?

5. How do you measure a snake?

Answers on next page

Answer 1. To cover their butt quacks

Answer 2. Address

Answer 3. Thunder pants

Answer 4. There always up to something

Answer 5. In inches they have no feet

> If you find these jokes rubbish
>
> Wreck them silly!

Copy this picture
Using your finger
And tomato sauce

Spill coffee or tea here

Wreck me silly!

oops

Poke holes in the faces
With a pencil!

Foot print goes here
(check for poo first)

Ok! You win a million pound!

SHOPPING LIST

Clothes
New bed
Car
Mansion

Your plane crashes on the way to Spain
You and your two friends survive
Friend 1... Mia
Friend 2... Frankie
There is no food on the island. Your absolutely
Starving. Your in a dilemma. The only way your going
To eat is by sacrificing a friend.
Which friend is going to be today's lunch?
Friend 1
Friend 2
How did you decide?

BURP!

(Don't worry friends
I wouldn't really eat you
I love you both)

Contacts

Name	Mobile	Email
Elaine	07730...	18Davidsoe1@olympustrust.co.uk
Dad (Ross)	07	rossdavidson83@hotmail.co.uk

Take a long look and draw that beautiful face!

Any resemblance?

Glue your pencil onto this pencil!

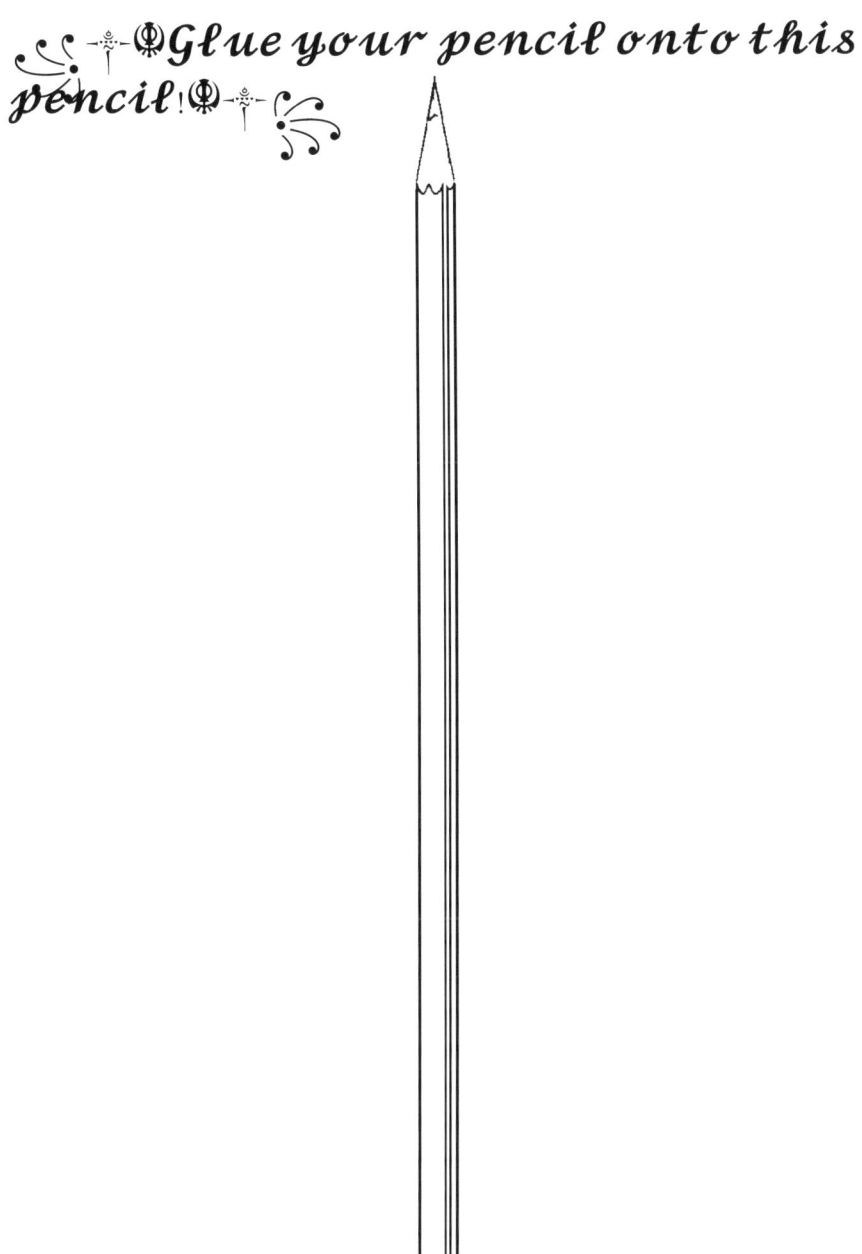

Glue and glitter
Glitter white parts only!

Dream Journal

Date: 30/10/21   Time: 21:00 pm

Thoughts Before Sleep

Emotions Before Sleep
Happy and tired.

Dream

Interpretation

Feeling Upon Awakening

Comments

Dream Journal

Date: 11/11/21   Time: 20:20

Thoughts Before Sleep

Is tommorow going 2 be good?

Emotions Before Sleep

happy and ?

Dream

Interpretation

Feeling Upon Awakening

Comments

Dream Journal

Date:_____   Time:_____

Thoughts Before Sleep

_____
_____
_____
_____

Emotions Before Sleep

_____

Dream

_____
_____
_____
_____
_____
_____

Interpretation

_____
_____

Feeling Upon Awakening

_____
_____
_____

Comments

_____
_____
_____

Dream Journal

Date:_____   Time:_____

Thoughts Before Sleep

Emotions Before Sleep

Dream

Interpretation

Feeling Upon Awakening

Comments

Dream Journal

Date:_____ Time:_____

Thoughts Before Sleep

_____
_____
_____
_____
_____

Emotions Before Sleep

_____

Dream

_____
_____
_____
_____
_____
_____
_____
_____

Interpretation

_____
_____
_____

Feeling Upon Awakening

_____
_____
_____

Comments

_____
_____
_____

Make your own story by filling in the blanks!

Walking through the forest, there is a ..clown..... in the distance. The forest floor Was muddy and dirty. We had to check our Shoes for ..poop........., because we were offered Refuge in the witches ..house... The witch Cackled and her face was full of ..mud............... Come in don't be afraid she whispered. "I won't Hurt you" I just want your....blood............. You gulp and glance to your friend. "omg I am .... myself". Your friend ...screams..... Agrees and pulls a face. Kind of like she is trying To keep a fart in. While the witch stirred the Cauldron, the girls took their chance and ran Like ..a....lion............ All the way home.

When they awoke and ate there ..poo........ They both giggled like ..farts.......... At their crazy Dream.

I plant a seed
It's the seed of love
I sit and watch it grow
from leaf to bud
from bud to blossom
we finally say hello

hello!

Rub the genie's Belly with talc!
Make 3 wishes

1. To be rich
2. To get my own car.
3.

Copy the following text. easy eh!! I forgot to tell you you must use your left hand.

I am beautiful and I am confident.
I am the best I can be and will always
Try my best in everything I do.
I am my own person, but will help my
Family and friends. Till the very end.

Your turn

I am beautiful and I am confident.

Squeeze a juicy orange into the jug

And try not to miss!!!!!

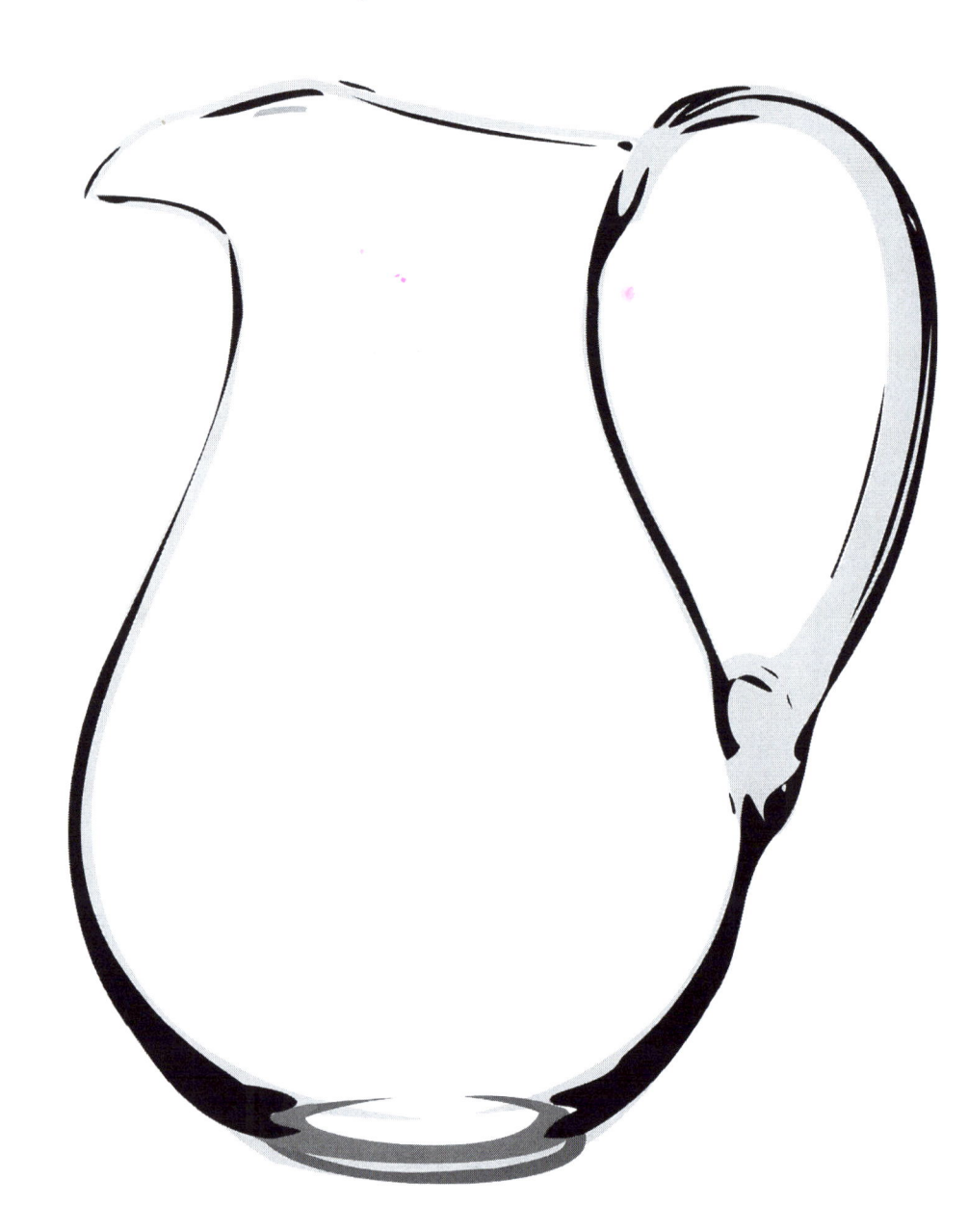

Your at a party and your friend falls to sleep
For a bit of fun you put lipstick, eye shadow
And foundation on his face.

You know what goes great with cake?

(Clue! It's yellow and gooey)

Make sure you cover the full cake!
YOU ARE A REAL DAMN REBEL!

15 point self reflection

1. Seven things that make you happy.
2. What are your weaknesses?
3. Your three biggest goals
4. What do you love about yourself?
5. Ten interesting facts about yourself
6. Things that make you laugh
7. How do you relax?
8. What am I thankful for?
9. Three things I do well
10. What are you passionate about?
11. What drains your energy?
12. What scares you?
13. Describe yourself in ten words
14. What are your strengths?
15. What is my saddest memory?

15 point self reflection
Your answers

friends, family ✓ ✓ ✓

1. Family, friends, food, drinks, clothes and my dressing table. My braclet.

2. I don't really know

3. To get my job, get my future I hope for. and be rich.

4. ?

5.

15 point self reflection
Your answers

6. ~~Mu~~ My friends

7. By listening to music.

8. Family and friends.

9. Singing

10.

15 point self reflection
Your answers

11. Nothing

12. Spiders and the ocean.

13. Shy,

14.

15.

Wreck this page silly!

BIG FAT BUM

Williggg

Billy

cheese

Stain this page!

Coffee

Colour in the octopus

Splatter any liquids you want here!

2021

JANUARY
S	M	T	W	T	F	S
					1	2
3	4	5	6	7	8	9
10	11	12	13	14	15	16
17	18	19	20	21	22	23
24	25	26	27	28	29	30
31						

FEBRUARY
S	M	T	W	T	F	S
	1	2	3	4	5	6
7	8	9	10	11	12	13
14	15	16	17	18	19	20
21	22	23	24	25	26	27
28						

MARCH
S	M	T	W	T	F	S
	1	2	3	4	5	6
7	8	9	10	11	12	13
14	15	16	17	18	19	20
21	22	23	24	25	26	27
28	29	30	31			

APRIL
S	M	T	W	T	F	S
				1	2	3
4	5	6	7	8	9	10
11	12	13	14	15	16	17
18	19	20	21	22	23	24
25	26	27	28	29	30	

MAY
S	M	T	W	T	F	S
						1
2	3	4	5	6	7	8
9	10	11	12	13	14	15
16	17	18	19	20	21	22
23	24	25	26	27	28	29
30	31					

JUNE
S	M	T	W	T	F	S
		1	2	3	4	5
6	7	8	9	10	11	12
13	14	15	16	17	18	19
20	21	22	23	24	25	26
27	28	29	30			

JULY
S	M	T	W	T	F	S
				1	2	3
4	5	6	7	8	9	10
11	12	13	14	15	16	17
18	19	20	21	22	23	24
25	26	27	28	29	30	31

AUGUST
S	M	T	W	T	F	S
1	2	3	4	5	6	7
8	9	10	11	12	13	14
15	16	17	18	19	20	21
22	23	24	25	26	27	28
29	30	31				

SEPTEMBER
S	M	T	W	T	F	S
			1	2	3	4
5	6	7	8	9	10	11
12	13	14	15	16	17	18
19	20	21	22	23	24	25
26	27	28	29	30		

OCTOBER
S	M	T	W	T	F	S
					1	2
3	4	5	6	7	8	9
10	11	12	13	14	15	16
17	18	19	20	21	22	23
24	25	26	27	28	29	30
31						

NOVEMBER
S	M	T	W	T	F	S
	1	2	3	4	5	6
7	8	9	10	11	12	13
14	15	16	17	18	19	20
21	22	23	24	25	26	27
28	29	30				

DECEMBER
S	M	T	W	T	F	S
			1	2	3	4
5	6	7	8	9	10	11
12	13	14	15	16	17	18
19	20	21	22	23	24	25
26	27	28	29	30	31	

Notes

Notes

Notes

Notes

Notes

Notes

Notes

Notes

Notes

Notes

Write the lyrics of your favourite song

Finish this face

Stab holes in each circle!

Hi there!

I'm writing this journal and was wondering if you were liking it?

If you are enjoying 5 stars would be super
If not pelt me with tomatoes!
(but you wouldn't want to do that)

Stir at this illusion for no reason!

As your tree
Of life
Expands
And your
Heart
Branches out
To the
Wonders of
The universe
And what
Love can
Bring about

Then you have gained your roots

Draw this heart with nail varnish

HIT THE BULLSEYE WITH SQUIRTY CREAM

How brainy are you?
(multiple choice)

1. **Who invented the telephone?**

   a. John craven

   (b.) Alexander graham bell ✓

   c. Eddie Cochrane

2. **Who invented the television?**

   a. Jim Bowen

   (b.) John logie Baird ✓

   c. Margaret thatcher

3. Who founded the apple company?

(a.) Steve jobs ✓

b. Bernard Clifton

c. John Lennon

4. The name of a shape with ten sides?

(a.) decagon ✓

b. octagon

c. pentagon

5. How many bones are in the human body?

a. 115

(b.) 206 ✓

c. 418

1. If you could be any animal what would it be?

   ......Bird..............................

2. Three things on your bucket list?

   ...New bed, a new wardrobe............

3. Strangest thing you have ever eaten?

   ...Doritos in pizza wrap....

4. What would you do on mars for fun?

   ...Make tik toks....................

5. When I dance I look like?

   ...A chicken.....................

6. On a scale 1-10. how cool are you?

   ......8.5........................

How brainy are you. answers

1. Alexander graham bell ✓

2. John logie Baird ✓

3. Steve jobs ✓

4. Decagon ✓

5. 206 ✓

How did you do?

5/5

Just a 99 ice cream because it is page 99

42 43 46
54 44 32

Write your own life story

WOULD YOU LIKE TO MAKE ME SOME YUMMY JAM ON TOAST

𓂀 You know what to do! 𓂀

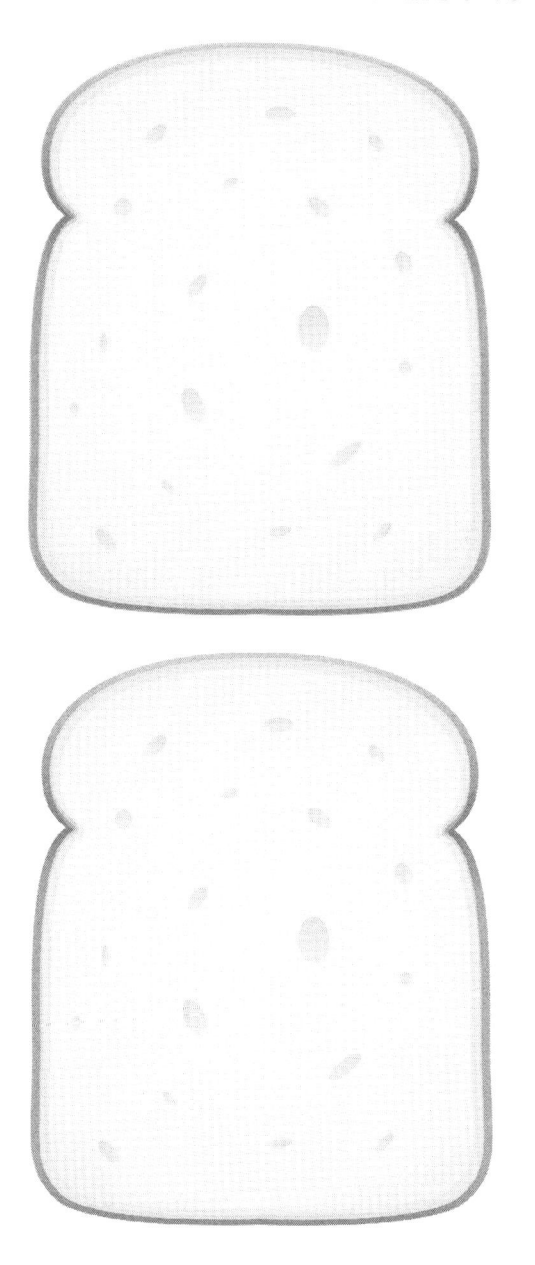

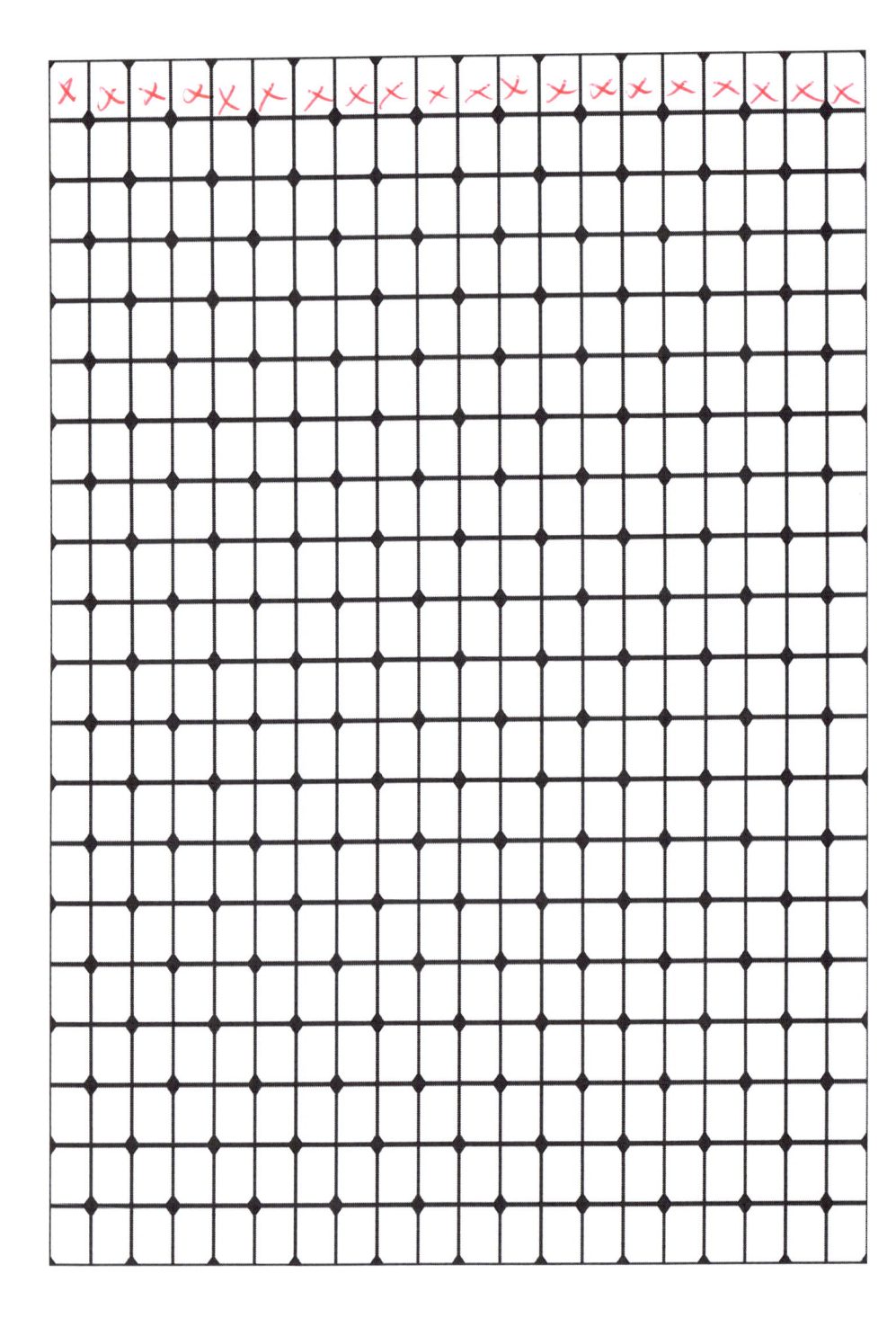

Put a red x in every box

This journal is coming to an end
Where do you see yourself in 5 years?

> I would be 20. I would be in college.

Have you ever hurt anybody?
be truthful!

> No I haven't.

You can always wreck it silly afterwards!

Name 8 best friends and why?

    2021   2023

1. Mia –   Ellie

2. Frankie –   maisie

3. Hollie –   maja

4. Phoebe –   liv

5. Maya –   Libby

6. Olivia –   Harry

7. Libby –   Kyle

8.   Dan

OH, yea. That reminds me could you smear some chocolate spread

Write a poem with the words..
Trousers, pig, house, crank, car.

Your doodle

Your doodle

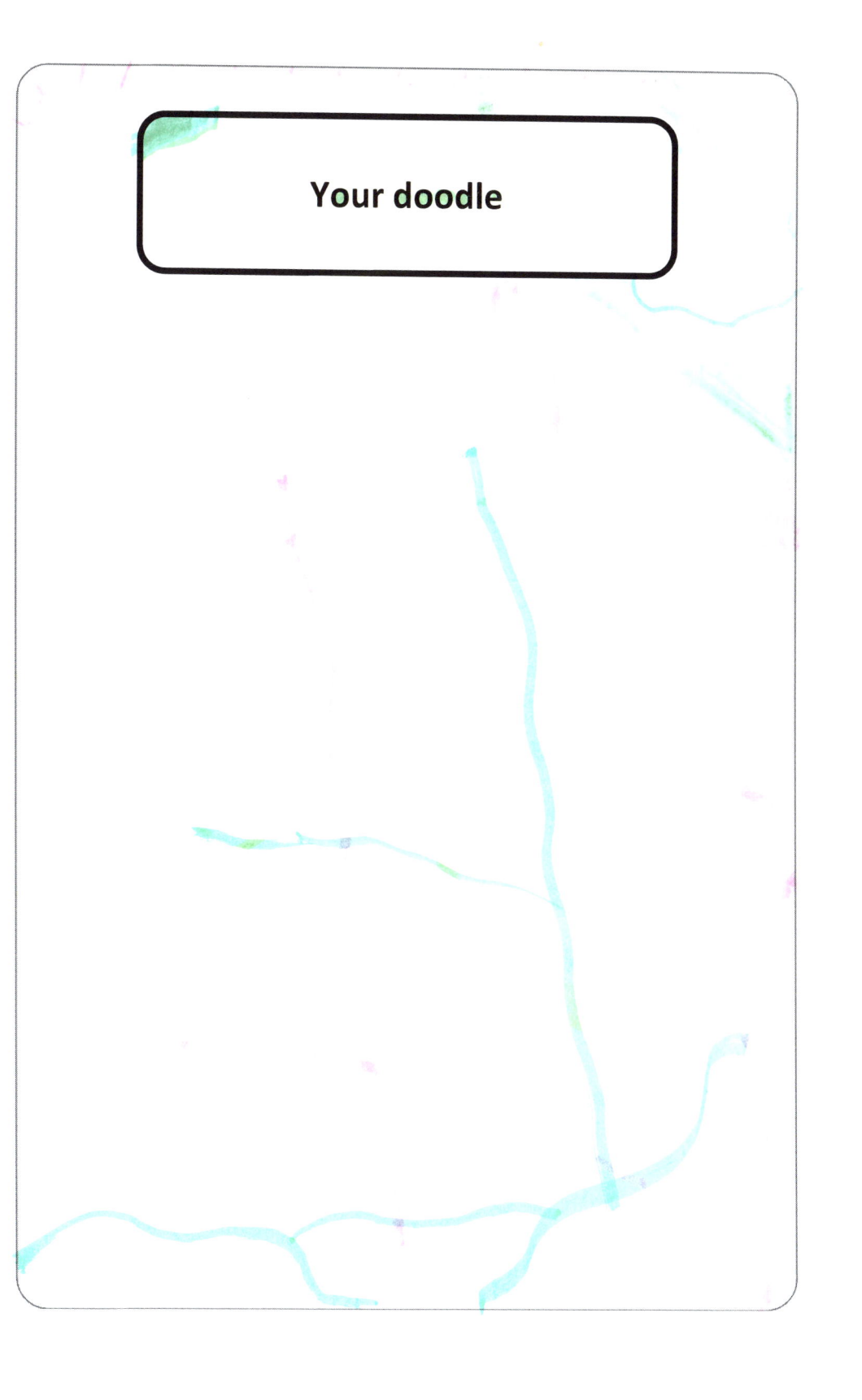

Your doodle

Your doodle

Your doodle

Your doodle

Your doodle

Your doodle

Well this is the end of the book.
I genuinely hope you had fun and
Made use of every page. I have many
More books on amazon. If you would
Like to have a look. We must all chase
our dreams. Thank you!

Thank you!
I loved the book!

Doodles

Printed in Great Britain
by Amazon